Montville Township Public Library
90 Horseneck Road
Montville, N.J. 07045-9626

<u>Library Hours</u>
Monday	10 a.m. - 9 p.m.
Tuesday	10 a.m. - 9 p.m.
Wednesday	1 p.m. - 9 p.m.
Thursday	10 a.m. - 9 p.m.
Friday	10 a.m. - 5 p.m.
Saturday	10 a.m. - 5 p.m.
Sunday	1 p.m. - 5 p.m.

Closed Sundays
Memorial Day through Labor Day

MOTORCYCLES

by Darlene R. Stille

Content Adviser: Pepper Massey-Swan, Director,
Sturgis Motorcycle Museum & Hall of Fame,
Sturgis, South Dakota

Reading Adviser: Dr. Linda D. Labbo,
Department of Reading Education, College of Education,
The University of Georgia

Compass Point Books

Minneapolis, Minnesota

Compass Point Books
3109 West 50th Street, #115
Minneapolis, MN 55410

Visit Compass Point Books on the Internet at *www.compasspointbooks.com* or e-mail your request to *custserv@compasspointbooks.com*

Photographs ©: Daniel Hodges, cover, 14, 16, 26 (right); Eric Hoffmann, 1, 10; David R. Frazier Photolibrary, 4, 8–9, 12; Hulton/Archive by Getty Images, 6; Richard T. Nowitz/Corbis, 18; Bob Krist/Corbis, 20; Unicorn Stock Photos/Joseph Sohm/ChromoSohm, 22; DigitalVision, 24; Richard Hamilton Smith/Corbis, 26 (left).

Editor: Christianne C. Jones
Photo Researcher: Svetlana Zhurkina
Designers: Melissa Kes/Jaime Martens

Library of Congress Cataloging-in-Publication Data
Stille, Darlene R.
  Motorcycles / by Darlene R. Stille.
      p. cm. — (Transportation)
Summary: A simple introduction to different kinds of motorcycles and how they are used.
Includes bibliographical references and index.
  ISBN 0-7565-0607-7 (hardcover)
  1. Motorcycles—Juvenile literature. [1. Motorcycles.] I. Title. II. Series.
  TL440.15.S75 2004
  629.227'5—dc22   2003012303

Table of Contents

NOTE: In this book, words that are defined in the glossary are in **bold** the first time they appear in the text.

Here Comes a Motorcycle

What's that coming down the road? It has one wheel in front and one wheel in back. It has handlebars and a seat in the middle. It is bigger than a bicycle and makes a strange noise. What is it? It's a motorcycle!

The First Motorcycles

In 1885, a German man named Gottlieb Daimler invented the first motorcycle. He put an engine on a bicycle made of wood.

People liked the new invention. Soon, people were making more modern motorcycles. Some people raced motorcycles. Others rode them for fun.

Some armies even bought motorcycles! Riders on the army motorcycles delivered messages during wartime.

◄ A motorcycle in 1908

What Makes a Motorcycle Go?

A gasoline **engine** starts the motorcycle. The rider pushes a button or the pedal to start the engine.

A **throttle** makes the motorcycle go. The throttle is on the end of a handlebar. Twisting the throttle makes the motorcycle go faster. Pushing the brakes makes the motorcycle stop.

Let's ride a motorcycle!

9

Dressing for a Ride

You need the right clothes to go on a motorcycle ride. The right clothes will keep you safe on your ride.

Put on a helmet to keep your head safe. Wear goggles or glasses to keep wind and dust out of your eyes. Wear heavy boots or shoes, gloves, and a heavy jacket and pants to protect your body. Now you are dressed for a motorcycle ride.

Riding a Road Bike

Vroom! Here we go! We're riding a road bike. Bike is a nickname for a motorcycle. Road bikes are for riding on smooth streets and roads. Some road bikes are big and heavy. Others are small and light. Road bikes can go as fast as a car.

Many people take vacations on road bikes. They put **saddlebags** on the side of the motorcycle. People pack clothes, water, sunblock, and other small items in the saddlebags.

Three-Wheelers and Sidecars

Look! We are passing a motorcycle with a sidecar. A sidecar is an attachment that has one wheel. Another passenger can ride in the sidecar.

Some motorcycles have three wheels. A three-wheeler has one wheel in front and two wheels in back. It also has a box between the two back wheels. A motorcycle with a sidecar is also a three-wheeler.

Custom Bikes

What kind of motorcycle is parked on that sidewalk? It has high handlebars and fancy paint. It has a wheel far out in front. The back wheel is low to the ground. It is a custom bike!

Some people make their own custom bikes. They use parts from different motorcycles. Each custom bike looks different.

Mopeds

Look! Now we are passing a moped. A moped is like a bicycle and a motorcycle put together. Mopeds have a motor like motorcycles and pedals like bicycles.

Mopeds cannot go as fast as motorcycles. They are smaller than motorcycles. Mopeds are good for short trips. They are popular all over the world!

Motor Scooters

Now we are passing a motor scooter. Motor scooters have two small wheels and a floor between the front and back wheels.

Some scooters only have one seat. Others have a passenger seat. There are also very small motor scooters that do not have a seat at all! You stand up when you ride these tiny scooters.

Police on Motorcycles

Wow! Two motorcycles pass us going very fast. Police officers are riding the motorcycles. The officers are chasing a speeding car.

Motorcycles help police **patrol** highways. They also help police get through busy city streets. Sometimes police officers ride motorcycles in parks, too.

Racing Motorcycles

People can race all kinds of motorcycles. Racing motorcycles have powerful engines. They are painted in bright colors.

People race road bikes on roads or racetracks. The tracks are round or oval shaped.

Off-road bikes race over muddy hills. Off-road bikes have special tires that can go over rough ground. Some off-road racers try to go fast. Others make their bikes jump high in the air.

▲ ATV

▲ Segway

ATVs and Segways

An ATV is an all-**terrain** vehicle. ATVs are often called four-wheelers. They have handlebars and big tires. ATVs can go over rough ground, bumpy hills, and snow.

A Segway has several electric motors. They are battery-powered. It also has two wheels. You stand on a base between the wheels. To make a Segway move, you hold the handlebars and lean forward, backward, or sideways.

All kinds of motorcycles are fun to ride.

Glossary

engine—a machine that changes energy into a force that causes motion

patrol—to walk around an area to protect it

saddlebags—bags that hang over the rear wheel of a motorcycle

terrain—an area of land or ground

throttle—a grip or lever that controls the vehicle's speed by controlling how much fuel or air flows into the engine

Did You Know?

* You need a special license to drive a motorcycle. You must pass a motorcycle driving test. Many states have free motorcycle driver education courses.

* Gottlieb Daimler not only invented gasoline motorcycles but also helped found the company that makes Mercedes-Benz cars.

* People in the United States and France tried to build motorcycles in the 1800s. They did not have gasoline engines. Instead, they put steam engines on bicycles.

* A stunt rider named Evel Knievel made many jumps with motorcycles. He jumped his motorcycles over cars, trucks, and buses. His biggest motorcycle jump was over 50 cars! He broke 35 bones in motorcycle crashes.

Want to Know More?

At the Library

Graham, Ian. *Superbikes.* Chicago: Heinemann Library, 2003.

Hendrickson, Steve. *Enduro Racing.* Mankato, Minn.: Capstone Press, 2000.

Henshaw, Peter. *The Encyclopedia of Motorcycles.* Philadelphia: Chelsea House, 2000.

Miller, Heather. *Motorcycles.* Chicago: Heinemann Library, 2003.

On the Web

For more information on motorcycles, use FactHound to track down Web sites related to this book.

1. Go to *www.compasspointbooks.com/facthound*
2. Type in this book ID: 0756506077
3. Click on the *Fetch It* button.

Your trusty FactHound will fetch the best Web sites for you!

Through the Mail

Sturgis Motorcycle Museum &
Hall of Fame

P.O. Box 602
Sturgis, SD 57785
Write to learn more about the history of motorcycles and the Sturgis Rally

On the Road

Motorcycle Hall of Fame Museum

13515 Yarmouth Drive
Pickerington, OH 43147
See a wide range of motorcycles on display

Index

About the Author

Darlene R. Stille is a science editor and writer. She has lived in Chicago, Illinois, all her life. When she was in high school, she fell in love with science. While attending the University of Illinois, she discovered that she also enjoyed writing. Today she feels fortunate to have a career that allows her to pursue both her interests. Darlene R. Stille has written more than 60 books for young people.